CELESTE
SAVES ✦ THE ✦ CITY

Written by Courtney Kelly, P.E.
Illustrated by Erin Nielson

Copyright © 2022 Courtney Kelly

All rights reserved. No part of this book may be reproduced in any form or by any electronic or mechanical means, including information storage and retrieval systems, without permission in writing from the publisher, except by reviewers, who may quote brief passages in a review.

www.courtneykellybooks.com

ISBN 978-0-578-31519-5 (Hardcover)
ISBN 978-0-578-35170-4 (Paperback)
ISBN 978-0-578-31520-1 (E-Pub)
Library of Congress Control Number 2022900034

Some events and places in this book are nonfictional. Readers are encouraged to research and learn more about them.

Edited by: Courtney Kelly
Cover, illustrations, and interior layout by: Erin Nielson

Courtney Kelly Books
Printed in the United States of America

Discount pricing is available for bulk orders (25 or more books). For more information, please contact us at info@courtneykellybooks.com

To my family, friends, and mentors. Thank you for believing in my bold, daring, and ambitious dreams. I am forever grateful for your support and guidance. I would not be who I am without you.

To the reader. May you always keep your eyes fixed upon your dreams. There will be twists and turns along the way, but stay the course. The path may be different than what you expect, but keep moving forward. One day you will look up and you will have arrived.

- Courtney Kelly

Celeste grew up in a city by the name of New Orleans.
Filled with lots of happy people, there was always a fun scene!

Tourists would ride bright red streetcars down blocks of mossy oak trees.

Beautiful horse-drawn carriages lined up outside the St. Louis Cathedral. It was quite a sight to see!

Rain would pour and waves would crash, filling the canals and lakes until it flooded the streets. But sometimes the water did not stop there and would rise to reach the tops of trees!

One day, a hurricane named Katrina roared and raged, inching closer and closer to town. Celeste and her family hurried to pack their things as the rain began coming down.

With tears in her eyes as she said goodbye to the only city she had ever known, they hopped into the truck to evacuate from the place they called home.

While looking out at Lake Pontchartrain, where the water seemed to touch the dark gray sky, Celeste told her dad, "When I grow up, I'll help New Orleans stay dry!"

"How will you do that?" her father then asked. Celeste quickly answered, "I will become a civil engineer to complete this task!"

Civil engineers design and build airports for planes, roads for cars, docks for boats, and railroads for trains. The Eiffel Tower, the Hoover Dam, the Panama Canal, and the Palm Islands of Dubai would not have been possible if civil engineers didn't give it a try.

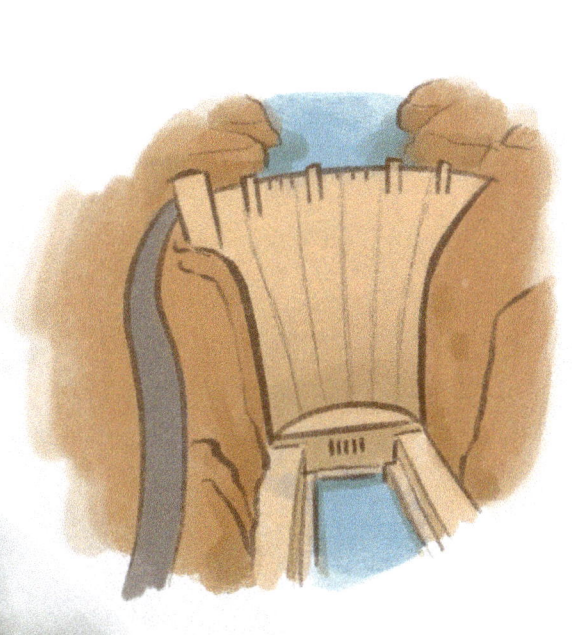

Celeste read and studied as much as she could.

For days and days, she thought of ways to keep water from flooding neighborhoods.

Suddenly, she realized that restoring wetlands was one way to succeed and could be a great place to start fulfilling her dream.

By building barrier islands surrounded by bald cypress trees in the lakes, people can work, eat, or play on their Louisiana-themed shapes.

Then, when storms come, the flood waters would be forced to slow down and the older wetlands can be kept safe and sound!

As the trees get bigger and grow more and more, they will become homes for fluffy and feathery animals galore. Catfish and frogs will be happy about this too, as they find a place to relax in nature just like me and you.

Celeste worked with an amazing team of people to bring her ideas to life.

Wearing a hard hat, boots, and safety vest, she toured each site with great pride.

Celeste continues to help other cities in need and with a little effort, there is no limit to what she can achieve.

What is your dream? When you grow up, what will you be?
The world will be watching and waiting to see!

About the Author

Born and raised in New Orleans, Louisiana, Courtney grew up wanting to be a veterinarian – until Hurricane Katrina changed the course of her life. After attending numerous engineering and math camps in high school, Courtney left Louisiana to pursue degrees in civil engineering and math at Southern Methodist University (SMU) in Dallas, Texas. She began a career in management of heavy civil infrastructure construction projects and went on to obtain a master's degree in civil engineering with a concentration in structures from SMU and an MBA from Lamar University in Beaumont, Texas. She is also a licensed professional engineer in the state of Texas. Courtney serves on the board for SOSMC USA, a nonprofit raising funds to renovate three flood-prone buildings on the campus of the Opportunity School for low-income disabled children in Chennai, India. In her spare time, she enjoys traveling, attending arts performances, and spending time with her fluffy bunny, Albus.

About the Illustrator

Erin Nielson is a freelance illustrator in McKinney, Texas. She loves to create imaginative and whimsical artwork, especially if that artwork can include a few animals. She has worked with clients such as BYU Independent Study, The Friend Magazine, and Cincinnati Children's Hospital. Erin's love of art started early, with her paintings and artwork hung in her grandmother's home. She attended college at Brigham Young University, and graduated with a BFA in illustration. Soon after graduating, she married her husband, Matt, and moved to Texas for new adventures. She now enjoys working out of her home studio with her daughter, Emma, and rescue dog Zoey.

CPSIA information can be obtained
at www.ICGtesting.com
Printed in the USA
LVHW071908090523
746527LV00006B/91